PUBLIC SPEAKING TO WIN!

T0106450

Also available in the Condensed Classics Library

A MESSAGE TO GARCIA
ACRES OF DIAMONDS
ALCOHOLICS ANONYMOUS
AS A MAN THINKETH
HOW TO ATTRACT GOOD LUCK
HOW TO ATTRACT MONEY
PUBLIC SPEAKING TO WIN!
SELF-RELIANCE
THE GAME OF LIFE AND HOW TO PLAY IT
THE KYBALION
THE LAW OF SUCCESS
THE MAGIC LADDER TO SUCCESS
THE MAGIC OF BELIEVING
THE MASTER KEY TO RICHES
THE MASTER MIND
THE MILLION DOLLAR SECRET HIDDEN IN YOUR MIND
THE POWER OF CONCENTRATION
THE POWER OF YOUR SUBCONSCIOUS MIND
THE SCIENCE OF BEING GREAT
THE SCIENCE OF GETTING RICH
THE SECRET DOOR TO SUCCESS
THE SECRET OF THE AGES
THINK AND GROW RICH
YOUR FAITH IS YOUR FORTUNE

PUBLIC SPEAKING TO WIN!

by Dale Carnegie

The Original Formula to Speaking with Power

Abridged and Introduced by Mitch Horowitz

THE CONDENSED CLASSICS LIBRARY

Published by Gildan Media LLC
aka G&D Media.
www.GandDmedia.com

Public Speaking to Win! was originally published in 1926 as
Public Speaking: A Practical Course for Business Men
G&D Media Condensed Classics edition published 2018
Abridgement and Introduction copyright © 2015 by Mitch
Horowitz

FIRST EDITION: 2018

Cover design by David Rheinhardt of Pyrographx

Interior design by Meghan Day Healey of Story Horse, LLC.

ISBN: 978-1-7225-0040-5

Contents

Introduction
The Power of What You Say 7

Chapter One
Developing Courage and Self-Confidence 11

Chapter Two
Self-Confidence Through Preparation 15

Chapter Three
Keeping Your Audience Awake 21

Chapter Four
The Secret of Good Delivery 25

Chapter Five
Platform Presence and Personality 27

CHAPTER SIX
How to Open a Talk................................... 31

CHAPTER SEVEN
How to Close a Talk................................... 33

CHAPTER EIGHT
How to Make Your Meaning Clear 37

CHAPTER NINE
How to Interest Your Audience 41

CHAPTER TEN
Improving Your Language........................... 45

CHAPTER ELEVEN
How to Get Action 47

ABOUT THE AUTHORS 53

The Power of What You Say

Nearly everything worth accomplishing in life comes down to communication. Your ability to sway others, win support, gain resources, succeed in your work, and correct injustice rests on your power of persuasion.

Even in our social-media age, the spoken word remains paramount. Candidates are elected because of what they say and how. Court trials hang on spoken testimony. Job interviews are face-to-face encounters. The same holds true for pitches to clients, donors, investors, customers, and financial backers. If you are seeking a career as a teacher, military officer, actor, broadcaster, or leader in any almost any field, your speaking ability is vital to your success.

Strikingly little has changed in human relations since Dale Carnegie wrote this guide to speaking in 1926, a decade before he gained international fame as the author of *How to Win Friends and Influence People*. When Carnegie produced this book he was making his living as the teacher of a popular seminar on public speaking. Carnegie had begun teaching his methods in 1912 at a YMCA in New York City. Requests for his course came in from around the country. By the mid-1930s, *Ripley's Believe-It-Or-Not* anointed Carnegie the king of public speaking with a cartoon reporting that he had personally critiqued 150,000 speeches.

Whether this is exaggerated, Carnegie's guide-book remains probably the best ever on how to speak with conviction and power. The book shows how to capture people's attention and win their confidence, whether you are speaking at a local club, a national sales conference, or in front of a class. But, as you will discover, this book delivers far more than instructions on how to give a good talk. Its greater value is that it teaches how to communicate effectively in virtually every sphere of life, on any occasion, and on behalf of any aim or purpose.

If you are a salesman, the book will help you will sell more. If you are a writer or editor, you will learn to better connect with readers. If you are an activist, you will find new ways to rally people to your cause.

What is the secret of Carnegie's formula? It comes down to three principles.

First, have an airtight knowledge of your subject—
know more than you need.

Second, when speaking, use plain language, personal examples, and tell stories of people.

Third, and finally, appeal to your listeners' sense of self-interest: We all crave safety, success, health, and prosperity. We also have a yearning for justice and fairness. Speak on these points, and you will likely bring people to your side.

Unless you are one of a very few naturally gifted speakers, implementing these simple guidelines requires persistence, inspiration, and strategy. You will find all of that—and more—in this book.

Carnegie's methods will bring you increased power. Use it for good ends.

—Mitch Horowitz

Chapter One

Developing Courage and Self-Confidence

Thousands of businessmen have taken my public-speaking courses. The vast majority have told me the same thing: "When I am called upon to stand up and speak, I become so self-conscious, so frightened, that I can't think clearly, can't concentrate, and can't remember what I wanted to say. I want to gain self-confidence, poise, and the ability to think on my feet."

Gaining self-confidence and courage, and the ability to think calmly and clearly while talking to a group, is not nearly as difficult as most imagine. It is not a gift bestowed by Providence. It is like the ability to play golf. Anyone can develop his own latent capacity, if he has sufficient desire to do so.

Rather than being frightened to speak publicly, you ought to think and speak *better* in front of a group. Their presence ought to lift and stir you. Many speakers will tell you that an audience is a stimulus, an inspiration that drives their brains to function more clearly, more keenly. At such times, thoughts, facts, and ideas that they did not know they possessed come to them. This will probably be your experience if you practice and persevere.

In order to get the most from this book, and to get it quickly, four things are essential:

FIRST

Start with a persistent desire. This is of far greater importance than you may realize. If I could look into your heart and mind right now, and ascertain the depth of your desires, I could foretell with near-certainty the swiftness of your progress. If your desire is pale and flabby, your achievements will be the same. But if you go after this subject with persistence, nothing will defeat you. Therefore, arouse your enthusiasm for this study. Think of what additional self-confidence and speaking ability will mean to you. Think of what it may mean in profits. Think of what it may mean socially—of the friends it will bring, of the increase of your personal influence, of the leadership it will give you.

SECOND

Know thoroughly what you intend to talk about. Unless a speaker has thought out and planned what he is going to say, he can't feel very comfortable when facing his auditors. An unprepared speaker *ought* to be self-conscious—and ought to be ashamed of his negligence.

THIRD

Act confident. "To feel brave," advises philosopher William James, "act as if we *were* brave, use all our will to that end, and a courage-fit will very likely replace the fit of fear." To develop courage when facing an audience, act as if you already have it. Unless you are prepared, of course, all the acting in the world will amount to little.

FOURTH

Practice! Practice! Practice! This is the most vital point of all. The first way, the last way, the never-failing way to overcome fear and develop self-confidence in speaking is—to speak. The whole matter finally simmers down to one essential: *practice*.

Chapter Two

Self-Confidence
Through Preparation

It has been my professional duty, as well as my pleasure, to listen to and criticize approximately six thousand speeches a year. Most were made by ordinary businesspeople. If that experience has engraved one thing on my mind it is this: the urgent necessity of preparing a talk before one starts to make it, and of having something clear and definite to say.

Aren't you unconsciously drawn to a speaker who you feel has a real message, which he zealously desires to communicate? That is half the secret of speaking. When a speaker is in that kind of mental and emotional state he will discover a significant fact: his talk almost makes itself. A well-prepared speech is already nine-tenths delivered. The one fatal mistake is neglecting to prepare. "Perfect love," wrote the apostle John, "casteth out fear." So does perfect preparation.

What is preparation? Reading a book? That is one kind, but not the best. Reading may help; but if one attempts to lift a lot of "canned" thoughts out of a book and give them out as his own, the whole performance will be lacking.

Does preparation mean pulling together some faultless phrases, written down or memorized? No. Does it mean assembling a few casual thoughts that really convey very little to you personally? Not at all.

It means assembling *your* thoughts, *your* ideas, *your* convictions, *your* urges. You have them everyday of your life. They swarm through your dreams. Your whole existence has been filled with feelings and experiences. These things are lying deep in your subconscious as thick as pebbles on the seashore. Preparation means thinking, brooding, recalling, selecting the ones that speak to you most, polishing them, working them into a pattern, a mosaic of your own. That doesn't sound so difficult, does it? It isn't. It just requires a little concentration and thinking to a purpose.

What topics should you speak on? Anything that truly interests you. Ask yourself all possible questions concerning your topic. For example, if you are to speak on divorce, ask yourself what causes divorce, what are the effects economically, socially, domestically? Should we have uniform divorce laws? Should divorce be more difficult? Easier?

When preparing a speech, assemble a hundred thoughts, and discard ninety. Collect more material than there is any possibility of using. Get it for that additional confidence it will give you, for that sureness of touch. Get it for the effect it will have on your mind and heart and whole manner of speaking. That is a basic factor of preparation—yet most speakers constantly ignore it.

You must practice your speaking. If you stand up and think clearly and keep going for two or three minutes, that is a perfect way to practice delivering a talk. Try this a few times. What you can do first on a small scale you can do later on a large scale.

When making your practice talk, do not attempt to tell us everything in three minutes. It can't be done. Take one, and only one, phase of your topic: expand and enlarge that. For example, you can tell us how you came to be in your particular business or profession. Was it due to accident or choice? Relate your early struggles, your defeats, your hopes, and your triumphs. Give us a human-interest narrative, a real-life picture based on first-hand experience. The truthful, inside story of almost anyone's life—if told modestly and without egotism—is sure-fire speech material.

Many wonder if they should use notes while speaking. As a listener, don't notes destroy about fifty percent of your interest in a talk? Notes prevent, or at least render difficult, a very precious intimacy that ought to exist between the speaker and the audience. They create an air of artificiality. They restrain an audience from feeling that a speaker has confidence, spontaneity, and power.

Make notes during your preparation—elaborate ones, profuse ones. You may wish to refer to them when you are practicing your talk alone. You may possibly feel more comfortable if you have them stored away in your pocket when facing an audience. But they should be emergency tools, used only in case of a total wreck.

If you *must* use notes while speaking, make them extremely brief and write them in large letters on an ample sheet of paper. Then arrive early where you are speaking and discretely place your notes on the lectern, or conceal them behind books on a table. Glance at them if you must, but be brief.

In a few limited instances it may be wise to use notes. Some people during their first few talks are so nervous that they are unable to remember what they wanted to say. In such cases, it is fine to hold a few very condensed notes in your hands.

Get comfortable with your talk. After you have thought it out and arranged it, practice it silently as you walk along the street. Also get off somewhere by yourself and go over it from beginning to end, using gestures, letting yourself go. Imagine that you are addressing a real audience. The more of this you do, the more comfortable you will feel when the time comes to deliver your talk.

CHAPTER THREE

Keeping Your Audience Awake

What is the secret of success? "Nothing great," said Ralph Waldo Emerson, "was ever achieved without enthusiasm." This quality is the most effective, most important factor in advertising, selling goods, and getting things done.

I once put considerable reliance on the *rules* of public speaking. But with the passing of years I have come to put more and more faith in the *spirit* of speaking.

Remember always that every time we speak we determine the attitude of our listeners. If we are lackadaisical, they will be lackadaisical. If we are reserved, they will be reserved. If we are only mildly concerned, they will be only mildly concerned. But if we are deadly in earnest about what we say, and if we say it with feeling and spontaneity and force and conviction, they cannot keep from catching our spirit to a degree.

So, to feel earnest and enthusiastic, stand up and *act* in earnest and *be* enthusiastic. Stop leaning against the table. Stand tall. Stand still. Don't rock back and forth. Don't bob up and down. Don't shift your weight from one foot to the other and back again. In short, don't make a lot of nervous movements. They proclaim your lack of ease and self-possession. Control yourself physically. It conveys a sense of poise and power. Fill your lungs with oxygen. Look straight at your audience. Look at them as if you have something urgent to say. Look at them with the confidence and courage of a teacher, for you *are* a teacher, and they are there to hear you and to be taught.

Use emphatic gestures. Never mind, just now, whether they are beautiful or graceful. Think only of making them forceful and spontaneous. Make them now, not for the sense they will convey to others, but for what they will do for *you*. And they will do wonders. Even if you are speaking to a radio audience, *gesture, gesture*. Your gestures won't, of course, be visible to the hearers, but the result of your gestures will be audible to them. They will give increased aliveness and energy to your tone.

I have made a special study of Abraham Lincoln as a public speaker. He is perhaps the most loved man

America has ever produced; and unquestionably he delivered some of America's greatest speeches. Although he was a genius in some ways, I am inclined to believe that his power with audiences was due, in large measure, to his sympathy and honesty and goodness. He loved people. "His heart," said his wife, "is as large as his arms are long." He was Christlike.

The finest thing in speaking is neither physical nor mental. It is spiritual. Jesus loved men and their hearts burned within them as He talked with them by the way. If you want a splendid text on public speaking, read your New Testament.

Chapter Four

The Secret of Good Delivery

We are often told to be natural, to be ourselves. But the same society that gives this advice often bleeds naturalness out of us by imposing all kinds of preconceptions of just what "naturalness" ought to be.

The problem of teaching or training people in delivery is not one of superimposing additional characteristics; it is largely one of removing impediments, of freeing people, of getting them to speak, albeit with a different vocabulary and judgment, as they did when they were four years old.

As you practice, if you find yourself talking in a stilted manner, pause and say sharply to yourself mentally: "What is wrong? Wake up. Be human." In the end, even the matter of delivery comes back to a point that has already been emphasized: namely, *put your heart in your talks.*

Here are four things that all of us do unconsciously and naturally in conversation. You should do them when speaking in public.

1. Stress the important words in a sentence and subordinate the unimportant ones. When you speak conversationally you naturally give emphasis to keywords, such as *ambition, affliction,* and *skyscraper.* But not to unimportant words, such as *the, and,* or *but.*

2. Allow the pitch of your voice to flow up and down the scale from high to low and back again—as the pitch of a little child does when speaking.

3. Vary your rate of speaking, running rapidly over the unimportant words, spending more time on the ones you wish to make stand out.

4. And, finally, pause before and after your important ideas.

This is exactly how you speak to your friends, coworkers, or spouse—and it is how you should address an audience.

CHAPTER FIVE

Platform Presence and Personality

*P*ersonality—with the exception of *preparation* and *ideas*—is probably the most important factor in public speaking. But personality is a vague and elusive thing. It is the whole combination of the man: the physical, the spiritual, the mental; his traits, his predilections, his tendencies, his temperament, his cast of mind, his vigor, his experience, his training, his life.

If you wish to make the most of your individuality, go before your audience well rested. A tired person is not magnetic or attractive. When you have to make an important talk, beware of your hunger. Eat as sparingly as a saint. Do nothing to dull your senses or energy.

To maintain high spirits in the room, make sure that your audience—whether it is large or small—is grouped closely together. No audience will be easily moved when it is scattered. Nothing so dampens enthusiasm as wide, open spaces and empty chairs between the listeners.

If you are going to talk to a small group, choose a small room. Better to pack the aisles of a small place than to have people dispersed through the lonely, deadening spaces of a large hall. If your hearers are scattered, ask them to move down front and be seated near you. Insist on this before you start speaking.

Unless the audience is a fairly large one, and there is a real reason, a necessity, for you to stand on a platform, do not do so. Get down on the same level with your listeners. Stand near them. Break up all formality. Get an intimate contact. Make the thing conversational.

Take a deep breath. Look over your audience for a moment. If there is a noise or disturbance, pause until it quiets down. Hold your chest high. But why wait until you get before an audience to do this? Do it daily in private life. Then you will do it unconsciously in public.

And what shall you do with your hands? Forget them. If they fall naturally to your sides, that is ideal. And this returns us to the much-abused question of gesture. A man's gestures, like his toothbrush, should be very personal things. As all of us are different, our gestures will be individual if only we act natural. No two people should be drilled to gesture in precisely the same fashion.

I can't give you rules for gesturing—and neither can anyone else. For everything depends on the temperament of the speaker, upon his preparation, his enthusiasm, his personality, the subject, the audience, the occasion. Above all, be truthful; be comfortable; be yourself.

CHAPTER SIX

How to Open a Talk

For some unfortunate reason, the novice often feels that he ought to be funny as a speaker. So he is inclined to open with a humorous story, especially if the occasion is an after-dinner affair. The chances are his stories don't "click." In the immortal language of Hamlet, they prove "weary, stale, flat, and unprofitable."

In the difficult realm of speechmaking, what is more difficult, more rare, than the ability to make an audience laugh? Remember, it is seldom the story that is funny. It is *the way it is told* that makes it a success. Ninety-nine people out of a hundred will fail woefully with the identical stories that made Mark Twain famous.

The second egregious blunder that the beginner is likely to make in his opening is this: He apologizes. "I am no speaker . . . I am not prepared to talk . . . I have nothing to say . . ." Don't! Don't! Why insult your audience by suggesting that you did not think them worth preparing for, that just any old thing you happened to have on the fire would be good enough to serve them? We don't want to hear your apologies. We are there to be informed and interested—to be *interested,* remember that.

Arouse your audience's curiosity with your first sentence—and you have their attention. An article in *The Saturday Evening Post* entitled "With the Gangsters," began: "Are gangsters really organized? As a rule they are. How?" With ten words the writer announced his subject, told you something about it, and aroused your curiosity.

Everyone who aspires to speak in public ought to study the techniques that magazine writers use to immediately hook the reader's interest. You can learn far more from them about how to open a speech than you can by studying collections of speeches.

CHAPTER SEVEN

How to Close a Talk

I f you want to know how to end a speech, you can do no better than study the close of Lincoln's Second Inaugural:

> *With malice toward none, with charity for all, with firmness in the right as God gives us to see the right, let us strive on to finish the work we are in, to bind up the nation's wounds, to care for him who shall have borne the battle and for his widow and his orphan, to do all which may achieve and cherish a just and lasting peace among ourselves and with all nations.*

You have just encountered what is, in my opinion, the most beautiful speech ending ever delivered. But you are not going to deliver immortal pronouncements as president in Washington or prime minister in Ottawa.

Your problem, perhaps, will be how to close a simple talk before a group of businessmen. How shall you set about it? Here are some suggestions.

FIRST

Even in a short talk of three to five minutes, a speaker is very apt to cover so much ground that at the close his listeners are a little hazy about all his main points. Some anonymous Irish politician is reported to have given this famous recipe for making a speech: "First, tell them what you are going to tell them; then, tell them; then, tell them what you told them." It is often highly advisable to "tell them what you told them." Briefly, of course, speedily—a mere outline, a summary.

SECOND

Try closing with a poetical quotation. If you can get a proper verse of poetry for your closing, it is almost ideal. It will give the desired flavor. It will give dignity. It will give individuality. It will give beauty. A choice Biblical quotation often has a profound effect.

THIRD

Build to a climax. The climax is a popular way of ending. It is often difficult to manage and is not an ending for all speakers or all subjects. But, when well done, it is excellent. It works up to a crest, a peak, getting stronger sentence by sentence. It often means ending with a tribute to someone or something, or an appeal for action—a topic we will cover in a future chapter.

CHAPTER EIGHT

How to Make
Your Meaning Clear

Napoleon's most emphatic instruction to his secretaries was: "Be clear! Be clear!"

When the disciples asked Christ why He taught the public by parables, He answered: "Because they seeing, see not; and hearing, hear not; neither do they understand."

And when you talk about a subject strange to your hearers, can you hope that they will understand you any more readily than people understood the Master?

Hardly. So what can we do about it? What did he do? He solved it in the most simple and natural manner imaginable: described the things people did not know by likening them to things they did know. The kingdom of Heaven . . . what would it be like?

"The kingdom of Heaven is like unto leaven . . . The kingdom of Heaven is like unto a merchant seeking goodly pearls . . . The kingdom of Heaven is like unto a net that was cast into the sea."

That was lucid; they could understand that. The housewives in the audience were using leaven every week; the fishermen were casting their nets into the sea daily; the merchants were dealing in pearls.

I once heard a lecturer on Alaska who failed, in many places, to be either clear or interesting because he neglected to talk in terms of what his audience knew. He told us, for example, that Alaska had a gross area of 590,804 miles.

Half-a-million square miles—what does that mean to the average person? Precious little. He is not used to thinking in square miles. They conjure up no mental picture. He does not have any idea whether half-a-million square miles are approximately the size of Maine or Texas. Suppose the speaker had said that the coastline of Alaska and its islands is longer than the distance around the globe, and that its area more than equals the combined areas of Vermont, New Hampshire, Maine, Massachusetts, Rhode Island, Connecticut, New York, New Jersey, Pennsylvania, Delaware, Maryland, West Virginia, North Carolina, South Carolina, Georgia, Florida, Mississippi, and Tennessee. Would that not give everyone a fairly clear conception of the area of Alaska?

If you belong to a profession that does technical work—if you are a lawyer, physician, engineer, or are in a highly specialized line of businesses—be doubly careful when you talk to outsiders to express yourself in *plain terms*, and to fill in necessary details.

Put your ideas into language plain enough for any boy to understand.

CHAPTER NINE

How to Interest
Your Audience

What would you say are the three most interesting subjects in the world? They are: *sex, property,* and *religion*. By the first we can create life, by the second we maintain it, and by the third we hope to continue it in the world to come.

But it is *our* sex, *our* property, and *our* religion that interests us. Our interests swarm around our own egos.

When a British newspaper baron was asked what interests people, he answered with one word: "themselves." Do you want to know what kind of person you are? Ah, now we are on an interesting topic. We are talking about *you.*

Remember that people spend most of their time, when they are not concerned with the problems of business, thinking about and justifying and glorifying themselves. The average man will be more wrought up over a dull razor than over a revolution in South America. His own toothache will distress him more than an earthquake in Asia destroying half-a-million lives. He would rather listen to you say some nice thing about him than hear you discuss the ten greatest men in history.

A successful magazine editor once told me the secret of capturing people's attention: "People are selfish," he said. "They are interested chiefly in themselves. They are not very much concerned about whether the government should own the railroads; but they do want to know how to get ahead, how to draw more salary, how to keep healthy, how to take care of their teeth, how to take baths, how to keep cool in the summer, how to get a job, how to handle employees, how to buy homes, how to remember, how to avoid grammatical errors, and so one. People are always interested in human stories, so I have some rich man tell how he made a million in real estate. I get prominent bankers and presidents of various corporations to tell their stories of how they battled their way up to power and wealth."

This editor has attracted millions of readers by appealing to their selfish interests.

But interest is also *contagious*. Your hearers are almost sure to catch it if you have a bad case of it yourself. A short time ago I heard a speaker warn his audience that if the present methods of catching rockfish in Chesapeake Bay were continued the species would become extinct. And in a very few years! He *felt* his subject. It was important. He was in real earnest about it. When he finished all of us probably would have been willing to sign a petition to protect the rockfish by law.

Always remember, your audience will feel interested in your topic to the degree that you are sincerely interested in it yourself.

CHAPTER TEN

Improving Your Language

The world judges us by four things: by what we do, by how we look, by what we say, and by how we say it.

Many people blunder through life with no conscious effort to enrich their stock of words, to master their shades of meaning, and to speak with precision. Many people habitually use the overworked and exhausted phrases of the office and street. Small wonder that their way of speaking lacks distinction and individuality.

But how are we to become intimate with words, to speak them with beauty and accuracy? Fortunately, there is no mystery about the means to be employed. *Books!* There is the secret. He who would enlarge his stock of words must drink deeply of good literature.

Lincoln wrote to a young man eager to become a successful lawyer: "It is only to get the books, and read and study them carefully . . . Work, work, work is the main thing."

What books? Begin with Arnold Bennett's *How to Live on Twenty-Four Hours a Day*. This book is as stimulating as a cold bath. It tells you a lot about that most interesting of all subjects—yourself. It reveals how much time you are wasting each day, how to stop the wastage, and how to use what you salvage.

To learn about greatness, make Ralph Waldo Emerson your daily companion. Command him first to give you his famous essay on "Self-Reliance." Read it again and again. Dedicate yourself to Emerson's essays and you will encounter some of the highest thoughts and finest uses of words in the English language.

Finally, don't use shopworn, threadbare words and expressions. Be exact in your meaning. Avoid trite comparisons such as "cool as a cucumber" or "high as a kite." Strive for freshness. Create expressions of your own. Have the courage to be distinctive.

CHAPTER ELEVEN

How to Get Action

If you could have the power of any talent that you now possess doubled and tripled, which one would you select? Wouldn't you likely designate your ability to influence others, to get action? That would mean additional power, additional profit, and additional pleasure.

Must this art—so essential to our success in life—remain forever a hit-and-miss affair? Must we blunder along depending upon our instinct, upon rule-of-thumb methods only? Or is there a more intelligent way to achieve it?

There is, and we shall discuss it at once—a method based on the rules of common sense, on the rules of human nature, a method that I have frequently, and successfully, used myself.

The first step in this method is to gain *interested attention*. Unless you do that people will not listen closely to what you say. We've already touched on some of the ways to do this: Talk to people about topics of vital interest—usually themselves. Be deeply in earnest about what you say. Be clear, plainspoken, and definite as to what you mean.

The second step is to gain the *confidence* of your hearers. Unless you do that, they will have no faith in what you say. And here is where many speakers fall down. Here is where many advertisements fail, where many business letters, many employees, many business enterprises go nowhere. Here is where many individuals fail to make themselves effective within the human environment.

The prime way to win confidence is to *deserve it.* I have noticed time without number that facile and witty speakers—if those are their chief qualities—are not nearly as effective as those who are less brilliant but more sincere. There is no use trying to pretend a sympathy or sincerity that one does not feel. It won't work. It must be genuine.

The second way to gain the confidence of the audience is to speak discretely out of your own experience. This helps immensely. If you give opinions, people may question them. If you relate hearsay or repeat what you have read, it may have a second-hand flavor. But what *you yourself have lived through*, that has a genuine ring of truth and veracity. And people like it. They believe it.

Once you have won people's confidence, consider what people are looking for—from you and from the world around them. One of the strongest of human motives is *the desire for gain.* And even stronger than the money motive is the desire for *self-protection.* All health appeals are based on that. To make an appeal to someone's sense of self-protection, make it personal. Don't, for example, quote statistics to show that cancer is on the rise. No. Tie it right down to the people who are listening to you, for example: "There are thirty people in this room. If all of you live to be forty-five, three of you, according to the law of medical averages, will die of cancer."

As strong as the desire for money—and for many even stronger—is the wish to be well regarded, to be admired. In other words, pride. Ask yourself why you bought this book. Were you influenced, to some extent, by the wish to make a better impression? Did you covet the flow of inward satisfaction that comes from making a commendable talk? Won't you feel a very pardonable pride in the power, leadership, and distinction that naturally flow to the good public speaker?

There is another powerful group of motives that influence us mightily. We shall call them religious motives. I mean religious not in the sense of orthodox worship or the tenets of any particular creed or sect. I mean rather that broad group of beautiful and eternal truths that Christ taught: justice and forgiveness and mercy, serving others and loving our neighbors as ourselves.

No man likes to admit, even to himself, that he is not good and kind and magnanimous. So we love to be appealed to on these grounds. It implies a certain nobleness of soul. We take pride in that.

To summarize all we have been discussing, here are the ways that you as a speaker can get people on your side and move them to action:

FIRST
Get interested attention.

SECOND
Win confidence by deserving it, not only by your sincerity but also by being qualified to speak on your subject, by telling us the things that experience has taught you.

THIRD
State your facts clearly and educate your audience regarding the merits of your proposal or cause.

FOURTH
Appeal to the motives that make us act: the desire for gain, self-protection, pride, pleasures, sentiments, affec-

tions, and religious ideals, such as justice, mercy, forgiveness, and love.

These methods, if used wisely, will not only help the speaker in public, but also in private. They will help him in the writing of sales letters, in constructing advertisements, in managing business interviews—and in making an impact in life.

About the Authors

Born in northwestern Missouri in 1888, DALE CARN-EGIE was one of the pioneers of motivational and self-help philosophy. World famous for his 1936 classic, *How to Win Friends and Influence People*, Carnegie began his career as a writer and teacher in 1912 when he offered courses on public speaking at a YMCA in New York City. Carnegie was one of the first business minds of the twentieth century to grasp the importance of being able to communicate ideas and concepts clearly to colleagues, coworkers, clients, and customers. His pioneering book, *Public Speaking: A Practical Course for Business Men*, from which this volume is abridged, first appeared in 1926. It is regarded as the seminal work on how to speak with power and skill. Carnegie died in New York City in 1955.

MITCH HOROWITZ, who abridged and introduced this volume, is the PEN Award-winning author of books including *Occult America* and *The Miracle Club: How Thoughts Become Reality*. *The Washington Post* says Mitch "treats esoteric ideas and movements with an even-handed intellectual studiousness that is too often lost in today's raised-voice discussions." Follow him @MitchHorowitz.

Printed in the USA
CPSIA information can be obtained
at www.ICGtesting.com
JSHW012046140824
68134JS00034B/3293